SCOTLAND

SECRETS OF THE HIGHLANDS

Managing Editor: Ruth Urbom

Editorial Assistant: Emma Agyemang

Creative Director: Alexander Rose

Jacket Design: Alex Ingr

Design Layout: Daniel Oliver

Art Editor: David Fraser

Production Manager: Carol Titchener

Sales & Editorial Manager: Karen Lomax

Author: Jessica Renison

Additional Material: Kaspa Hazlewood

ISBN 13: 978-0-7607-9234-6

ISBN 10: 0-7607-9234-8

A catalog record for this title is available from the Library of Congress

Printed and bound in Singapore

1 3 5 7 9 10 8 6 4 2

SCOTLAND

SECRETS OF THE HIGHLANDS

JESSICA RENISON

k

Kandour Ltd

Contents

Castles and Clans

The formidable families who ruled the Highlands and the magnificent fortress homes that are their legacy

The Gaelic language brings us the word "clan," meaning "children of the family." Back in the dark mists of the 13th century, the Highlands of Scotland were ruled by the clans, the great families of the nation.

The Highlands were entirely separate from the rest of Scotland in terms of their language and customs. The clans owned great tracts of land, based around a castle or manor, which they farmed to provide for their own. Each clan had a chief at its head, who was both law-giver and protector. Although the different clans often warred among themselves—cattle theft and territorial disputes were particularly widespread—when gathered together against a common enemy, the Highland clans were

powerful enough to challenge the authority of the crown of England. Gatherings of the clans were both social events and political assemblies.

The Scottish people still retain a strong link to their ancestral clans. Some, such as the Campbells and the Donalds, trace their ancestry back to figures in Celtic mythology. In reality, the clan chiefs were warlords with Norse, Norman, and Flemish blood, as well as Scottish and English, and their business was seizing territorial control for their families.

The chiefs kept court in much the same way as monarchs of the time. They employed a vast retinue of servants, and within their own territory, their word was law. Though renowned for their ruthlessness and

brutality, the clan chiefs left behind a marvelous legacy. Bards in the service of the chiefs composed epic poems celebrating the glorious victories of their people and recording the nation's history, and the magnificent castles that were their strongholds still grace the land to this day. Thus they are responsible for much of Scotland's cultural richness.

The castles scattered around Scotland—some bare ruins, others immaculately restored—all harbor the ghosts of clansmen past, and all have their special tale to tell. Their bluff stone walls have witnessed some of the most colorful and some of the bloodiest episodes in history and, here and there, remnants of these turbulent past times survive within to tell their tales.

*In 1719, when English forces attacked the castle,
the resident MacRae decided to blow it up himself,
rather than let it fall into English hands.*

Eilean Donan Castle

From its iron portcullis to its oak-beamed Banqueting Hall complete with piper's gallery, Eilean Donan Castle in the West Highlands is in every respect the quintessential Scottish castle. Set on an island at the meeting place of two lochs, and flanked by steep mountains on either side, its site reveals traces of an Iron Age fortification, evidence that it has long been used as a place of refuge in times of danger. Archaeological remnants left by its Iron Age settlers include the impression of a human foot stamped in the stone outside the castle.

A castle was first built on the site by King Alexander II in 1220 as a safe haven from the invading Vikings. During the 14th and 15th centuries, the Ross and the Mackenzie clans wrangled bitterly over ownership of Eilean Donan. At one point,

Euphemia, Countess of Ross, proposed marriage to the charming young Alexander Mackenzie in an attempt to gain possession of the castle, but he refused and for this insult was imprisoned by his would-be wife. The castle later fell into the hands of the MacRae clan, whose family seat it remains up to the present day. The castle built by Alexander II was destroyed, however, in the 18th century. The story goes that when, in 1719, English forces attacked the castle, the resident MacRae decided to blow it up himself, rather than let it fall into English hands and become a garrison for their troops, so he put a match to the storeroom of gunpowder in the fort, reducing the castle to ruins.

In its long and colorful history, Eilean Donan has had various famous names attached to it. Among the

many treasures in the castle's care is a letter from Bonnie Prince Charlie, dated 1745, summoning the clans to a gathering, and with it a lock of his hair. It also provided refuge to Robert the Bruce, future King of Scotland, whilst he was in flight from the English. Eilean Donan was rebuilt in 1932 according to architectural plans which came to one of the MacRae family in a dream; remarkably, these proved to be uncannily faithful to plan drawings of the original castle which have since been found. The picturesque castle is a favorite of artists and photographers, as well as being a popular place to get married, owing to its idyllic setting and romantic charm. It has also appeared in several movies, including *Highlander*, which starred Sean Connery.

Left: The impressive
façade of Edinburgh
Castle rises above
the city

Back in the dark mists of the 13th century,
the Highlands of Scotland were ruled by the clans,
the great families of the nation.

Edinburgh Castle

Edinburgh Castle is perhaps the most famous castle, not only in Scotland, but in the entire United Kingdom. The situation of the city makes it an ideal fortress, nestled as it is between sea and hills, and the castle itself sits on a steep rock at the city's highest point, commanding a spectacular view over the surrounding country. Its formidable façade is visible for miles around and it gives the impression that it has simply grown out of the rock as it reaches into the sky, some 260 feet (80 m) above the rest of the city. The Castle exudes all the noble grandeur befitting a seat of kings, but it has always been far more than a mere royal residence, and has in truth more often provided sanctuary and refuge to the harassed and hounded Scottish monarchs.

Although it has been a fortress since pre-Roman times, it first became a royal keep in the 12th century,

during the reign of David I. There was much wrangling over the Castle between the English and the Scots, and it passed from one crown to the other over subsequent centuries, but it was firmly back in Scottish hands by the time of James III of the Stewart dynasty, who made it his permanent palace and greatly expanded its scope.

Edinburgh Castle has played an important part in the history of its nation: it was here that in 1566 Mary, Queen of Scots, gave birth to the son who was to become King James VI of Scotland and King James I of England, uniting for the first time the crowns of those two warring countries. The Castle also harbors within its grounds the oldest building in the city: the miniature St. Margaret's Chapel, a delicate Norman edifice which has stood the test of time, surviving all the attacks which have reduced the rest of the castle to rubble to remain

Right: The Castle with Waverley train station in the foreground. A fine example of Victorian architecture, the station is the result of an amalgamation in 1868 of three stations originally built on the site of a drained loch. It is an elegant structure with an elaborate domed glass ceiling in the ticket hall. The name "Waverley" was taken from the Waverley novels of the famous Victorian writer Sir Walter Scott, and a monument of Scott greets passengers at the station entrance.

Guards still keep night watch to protect the crown jewels, all of which are fashioned of solid gold, encrusted with diamonds, pearls, and other precious gemstones.

standing some 900 years after it was built. Edinburgh Castle is one of the many castles throughout history that the Scottish people have destroyed themselves rather than let them fall into English hands. Before the 14th century battle of Bannockburn, Robert the Bruce ordered its destruction for fear that Edward II would triumph and seize the castle for the English. In the event, he defeated Edward II, but by then it was too late—the castle was no more.

Not surprisingly, given its long and hallowed history, the castle prizes its traditions. The One O'Clock Gun is still fired every day (except Sundays) to mark the time, a custom which has its origins in the days before reliable timepieces, when the gun was fired to allow sailing ships in the Firth of Forth to check the accuracy of their chronometers. It is the same sense

of long tradition which prompts hundreds of regiments from the world's armed forces to flock annually to the castle's Esplanade in a grand celebration of military music and marching. Indeed, an active military presence remains in the Castle to this day: the Army School of Piping has its home here and as late as the 1980s a tunnel had to be bored through the castle rock so that military personnel could gain access to the Castle without startling tourists.

Among the Castle's many curiosities is an iron fountain embedded in a wall of the Esplanade. It is known as the Witches' Well due to the rather unpleasant fact that it marks the spot where, in darker days, women found guilty of witchcraft were burned at the stake. It is also the home of the Scottish crown jewels. The royal crown, scepter and sword,

known as the Honors of Scotland, were discovered by the writer Sir Walter Scott in 1818 in an obscure locked room in the castle dungeons. Guards still keep night watch at the gatehouse with the sole purpose of protecting the crown jewels, all of which are fashioned of solid gold, encrusted with diamonds, pearls, and other precious gemstones. Perhaps its most treasured possession, though, is a more humble stone—not just any stone, but the Stone of Destiny, also known as the Stone of Scone. It was upon this stone that Scottish monarchs were once crowned. The stone, such a precious part of the Scottish heritage, was returned to Edinburgh Castle from Westminster Abbey in 1996 after many years' absence, on the understanding that it would be returned to the Abbey for future royal coronations.

Imposing and awe-inspiring, the Castle dominates Edinburgh's skyline

*Left:The flag of St.
Andrew flies from the
turrets of Inveraray
Castle*

*The Campbell clan motto "Ne Obliviscaris:
Do not forget" has overtones of a grim-faced
determination which is in keeping with their
fierce attachment to the family name.*

Inveraray Castle

Inveraray Castle has been the family seat of the Dukes of Argyll, who belong to Clan Campbell, one of Scotland's most fearsome and most respected clans, since the 1400s. The Castle is a unique blend of architecture, which includes the Baroque, Palladian, and Gothic styles. It was most recently restored in the 1970s by the current Duke's father following a devastating fire. Its four turrets, topped by conical spires, give it the look of a fairytale castle; the turbulent fortunes of its inhabitants, however, have been anything but a fairytale.

In medieval times, the Campbells were reviled by the other Highland clans due to their support of the Crown. They were related by marriage to King Robert the Bruce and as such had their feet in two camps, a situation which proved increasingly uncomfortable and made them far from popular among their fellow clansmen. Over the years, the family has fallen in and out of favor. The 8th Earl of Argyll was executed for supporting Oliver Cromwell against King Charles II, which proved to be a tactical error. The 10th Earl of Argyll raised a regiment for the Crown which was subsequently commanded to carry out the infamous Massacre of Glencoe, when the rebellious Highland clans were quelled in the most brutal way. This act was interpreted as one of clan vengeance, bringing about the further rejection and alienation of the family.

The Campbell clan motto, "*Ne Obliviscaris:* Do not forget" has overtones of a grim-faced determination which is very much in keeping with their fierce attachment to the family name. Perhaps quite aptly, considering the Campbell reputation for martial strength and their struggles with torn loyalties, there is an impressive array of weaponry on display in the Castle's magnificent Armory, most of it supplied by the British government.

" *Beautiful, glorious Scotland, has spoilt me for every other country!* **"**

Mary Todd Lincoln, US First Lady

Inveraray Castle's formidable façade, flanked by fir trees

Left: Dunnottar's impressive clifftop position

Dunnottar Castle

Perched on a perilous cliff which juts out into the North Sea, the ruins of Dunnottar Castle are whipped relentlessly by violent winds and echo with the tireless crashing of waves. Its awe-inspiring position means that it can act both as a remote haven and an ideal vantage point from which to attack. Dunnottar as it stands today is more than just a castle: its eleven buildings include barracks, stables and storehouses, making it easy to imagine the bustling activity of everyday medieval life within its crumbling walls. Most prominent among these buildings, and immediately commanding the eye with its cannon-blasted walls, is the 14th-century Tower House.

Dunnottar Castle has seen many a bloody day in its turbulent history. It was here that William Wallace set fire to an early wooden castle that stood on the site while it was occupied by English troops. And it was here that a small but determined garrison of Scots managed to preserve the Scottish Crown Jewels intact while Oliver Cromwell's army battered at its walls

for eight long months. The story of how it happened is one of the most prized in Scottish history.

Dunnottar was the family seat of the Earls Marischal of Scotland, whose function it was to protect the Scottish Crown Jewels, known as the "Honors of Scotland." After the execution of Charles I, King of England and Scotland, by Oliver Cromwell in 1649, the King's son took refuge in Scotland, and from there attempted to seize back the crowns of England and Scotland. When Oliver Cromwell discovered the whereabouts of the King's son, he promptly invaded Scotland to root him out. Cromwell had already destroyed the English crown jewels and was determined to get his hands on the Scottish crown jewels to purge the nation once and for all of the tainted trappings of monarchy. Charles II was hurriedly crowned at Scone while Cromwell advanced apace, but the crown jewels could not be returned to their rightful home in Edinburgh Castle because it was already occupied by Cromwell's troops, so the King commanded

that the Earl Marischal keep them safe at Dunnottar Castle. A group of 70 men managed to withstand Cromwell's attack on the castle for eight months, and when his cannon fire finally brought the walls down, they had already smuggled the royal crown, scepter, and sword out of the castle by lowering them down the cliff face into the safe hands of a servant woman who was pretending to gather seaweed. From there they traveled via a minister's bed to their burial place within a nearby church, where they remained for the next 10 years. In this way, the castle has secured its place in Scottish history as the protector of the nation's most precious emblems of sovereignty.

Dunnottar Castle has passed between English and Scottish hands several times over the years, and various notable figures, such as William Wallace and Mary Queen of Scots, have made the castle their home for a time; more recently it played host to the movie star Mel Gibson, who filmed his 1990 version of *Hamlet* here.

Dunnottar Castle in Stonehaven, on the east coast of Scotland

*Craigmillar Castle's most dubious claim to fame
is that Helen Duncan, the last woman to be convicted
of witchcraft in Britain, lived here.*

Craigmillar Castle

Craigmillar, situated three miles from Edinburgh, is one of the most beautifully preserved medieval castles in Britain. Its name comes from the Gaelic *Crag Maol Ard*, meaning "high bare rock." Though from the outside it may appear to be in ruins, its medieval spirit lives on in details such as the compact storerooms and intricate dovecote, which remain intact and allow the visitor a glimpse of life in simpler, if harsher, times. Indeed, now that local pigeons have moved into the dovecote, their noise and smell make it an even more realistic re-creation of life in medieval times!

At its center is the early 15th century Tower House, the work of Sir George Preston, a member of one of Edinburgh's most renowned families. His grandson, Sir William Preston, later added a curtain wall, creating an inner courtyard around the Tower House whose tree-shaded tranquility is one of the castle's most notable features. The castle is most remarkable for the extent to which its skeleton structure survives: its walls and floors and skillfully constructed stone vaulting are all more or less in place.

During the 16th century, Mary Queen of Scots stayed at the castle on several occasions, and it was during one of her stays that conspirators plotted to kill her husband Lord Darnley, whose disreputable lifestyle was making him a liability. They called their plot the "Craigmillar Bond."

The Preston family sold the castle in 1660 to the Gilmour family, who eventually found that castle life did not enable them to live in the luxurious manner to which they were accustomed, so they abandoned the castle to its fate. Craigmillar fell into ruin over the next two centuries and it was not until 1946 that it was rescued and restored by Historic Scotland, the government organization that preserves and promotes Scotland's heritage.

Aside from the castle, Craigmillar itself was once seen as little more than a slum and even today is blighted by poor living conditions. It consists largely of public housing, with very few shopping or leisure facilities, and it was the scene of angry riots in the 1980s. Perhaps its most dubious claim to fame, and one which sums up its grim reputation, is that Helen Duncan, the last woman to be convicted of witchcraft in Britain, lived here. However, valiant efforts have been made in recent years to clean up its reputation, and the creation of the Craigmillar Festival Society in 1976, which encourages artistic enterprise in the area, has gone a long way toward lifting the spirits of a once-downtrodden suburb.

Stirling Castle

Sitting high on a volcanic rock, surrounded by sea on three sides and keeping a watchful eye on the lowest crossing point of the River Forth, it is easy to see why the magnificent Stirling Castle is unrivaled in its strategic position. This enviable position has made the Castle the subject of much attention, both welcome and otherwise, over the years, as powerful men have sought to command its vantage point. Indeed, Stirling Castle has witnessed some of the great turning points in Scottish history: the infant Mary Queen of Scots was crowned here; her son, the future James IV of Scotland and I of England, was baptized here and then went on to hold his first Parliament as king in the Castle's Great Hall. It is even thought that the legend of King Arthur's Camelot is set within these splendid turreted walls, but to prove as much would be a difficult task.

As with many Scottish castles, Stirling has been tossed back and forth between the English and Scottish, either in conquest or as part of a bargain, or occasionally even as a gesture of goodwill. It was at Stirling that in 1291 the Scottish nobility first swore their allegiance to the English crown, under some duress from King Edward I. However, six years later William Wallace led the Scots to victory at the Battle of Stirling Bridge, and Stirling Castle was surrendered back to the Scots. The following year, another battle catapulted the Castle back into English hands, and the year following that, Robert the Bruce seized it back from the English. This pattern was repeated throughout the 14th century: all in all, the Castle's much-battered walls suffered 16 sieges.

It is hardly surprising, then, that the Castle has seen its fair share of trauma and tragedy over the years. But the traditional wrangling between English and Scots aside, there are other more tragic tales in its troubled history. James II murdered one of his earls within the castle walls, and James III was murdered by an unknown hand during a revolt against him led by his own son. But perhaps the most memorable, and certainly the most eccentric story connected with the Castle is one that has tragicomic overtones. In 1507, the alchemist employed by James IV (in the days when kings still employed alchemists) fell from the castle walls while attempting to fly to France using wings made of hen feathers.

Many songs and poems have been written celebrating William Wallace's victory at the Battle of Stirling Bridge in 1297. The following is taken from a marching song by William Sinclair:

To Scotland's ancient realm,
Proud Edward's armies came;
To sap our freedom and overwhelm
Our martial forces in shame.
"It shall not be!" brave Wallace cried
"It shall not be!" his chiefs replied!
"By the name our fathers gave her,
Our steel shall drink the crimson stream,
We'll all her dearest right redeem,
Our own broadswords shall save her."

All o'er the waving broom,
In chivalry and grace,
Shone England's radiant spear and plume
By Stirling's rocky base.
And stretching far beneath the view,
Proud Cressingham, thy banners flew.
When like a torrent rushing,
O God! From right and left the flame
Of Scottish swords like lighting came,
Great Edward's legions crushing.

High praise, ye gallant band,
Who in the face of day,
With daring hearts and fearless hands
Have cast your chains away.
The foemen fell on ev'ry side,
In crimson hues the Forth was dyed.
Bedew'd with blood the heather,
While cries triumphant shook the air,
Thus shall we do, shall we dare,
Wherever Scotsmen gather.

Above: Stirling Castle

*" We walked up to the house and stood some minutes
watching the swallows that flew about restlessly,
and flung their shadows upon the sunbright walls
of the old building. "*

*Dorothy Wordsworth
"Recollections of a Tour made in Scotland" (1803)*

Neidpath Castle

Neidpath is a medieval castle set in Border Country overlooking the river Tweed, near the town of Peebles. It has an L-shaped tower with walls built of rubble; it has roofed battlements and a balustraded balcony which acts as the sentry walk. Some original medieval features still survive, most notably the pit dungeon and the iron window bars.

Neidpath has been the seat of the Fraser, Douglas, and Hay clans over the years. The emblems of the Frasers and the Hays can still be found decorating the walls of the Castle gardens: strawberries for the Frasers and a goat's head for the Hays.

Neidpath was attacked by Oliver Cromwell's men in the 18th century, and apparently it held out longer than all the other Southern castles before its walls finally crumbled under his cannon fire. But aside from its military history, the Castle also boasts literary connections *and* has its very own ghost! Neidpath was visited by the Romantic poet William Wordsworth and by the novelist Sir Walter Scott, who became intrigued by its resident ghost, the "Maid of Neidpath." Jean Douglas, the daughter of William Douglas, Earl of March, was forbidden to marry the man she loved because he was below her social station. When he was sent away, she pined and wasted away to such a degree that when her lover returned to claim her, he did not recognize her. This was the final, devastating blow and Jean Douglas died of a broken heart. Her ghost, dressed in a long brown dress with a wide white collar, still stumbles through the Castle, mourning her lost love.

Left: Neidpath Castle in Peeblesshire

Behold her, single in the field,
Yon solitary Highland lass!

William Wordsworth,
'The Solitary Reaper'

"The Maid of Neidpath"
by Sir Walter Scott

O lovers' eyes are sharp to see,
And lovers' ears in hearing;
And love in life's extremity
Can lend an hour of cheering.
Disease had been in Mary's bower,
And slow decay from mourning,
Though now she sits on Neidpath's tower
To watch her love's returning.

All sunk and dim her eyes so bright,
Her form decay'd by pining,
Till through her wasted hand, at night,
You saw the taper shining;
By fits, a sultry hectic hue
Across her cheek was flying,
By fits, so ashy pale she grew,
Her maidens thought her dying.

Yet keenest powers to see and hear
Seem'd in her frame residing;
Before the watch-dog prick'd his ear,
She heard her lover's riding;
Ere scarce a distant form was kenn'd,
She knew, and waved to greet him;
And o'er the battlement did bend,
As on the wing to meet him.

He came—he passed—an heedless gaze,
As o'er some stranger glancing;
Her welcome, spoke in faltering phrase,
Lost in his courser's prancing.
The castle's arch, whose hollow tone
Returns each whisper spoken,
Could scarcely catch the feeble moan
Which told her heart was broken.

31

Cannons on the battlements of Culzean Castle

Above: Culzean Castle
Right: Dirleton Castle

Culzean Castle

Culzean Castle (pronounced "Cullane") is a relatively modern castle, designed in the 18th century by Robert Adams. This luxurious Georgian castle, complete with a circular saloon overlooking the sea and a grand oval staircase, was built for David Kennedy, Earl of Cassillis. It stands on the Ayr coast looking out towards the mist-covered mountains of the Isle of Arran.

When the Kennedy family handed the Castle over to the National Trust for Scotland, they made it a condition that the top floor should be given over to General Eisenhower as a mark of gratitude from the Scottish people. The President visited the Castle four times, making particular use of it during his retirement, when he was free to relax in its beautiful surroundings and enjoy painting, walking, and playing golf in its spacious grounds.

Dirleton Castle

The Scottish flag flies from the roof of Dirleton Castle. The well-preserved ruins of Dirleton Castle are well and truly hidden from the public eye among the dense trees and shrubs of Dirleton Gardens. The Castle is a complex structure with some of its medieval aspects beautifully intact, including the beehive-shaped dovecote, the arched gatehouse, the chapel, and the dank dungeon prison.

Left: Newark Castle,
Port Glasgow.

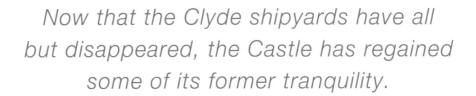

Now that the Clyde shipyards have all but disappeared, the Castle has regained some of its former tranquility.

Newark Castle, Port Glasgow

The substantial walls of Newark Castle face the River Clyde at Port Glasgow, which today affords it a beautiful riverside setting, but it was not always this way. The port was created here in 1668 when it proved too problematic to cut a deep enough channel up the Clyde to the city of Glasgow itself. As a result, far from being remote and isolated, Newark Castle was forced to share its home with ships and cranes, surrounded by the clanking industry of dock life. It was a far cry from the idyllic charm of the castles raised aloft on desolate rocks. Now that the Clyde shipyards have all but disappeared, however, the Castle has regained some of its former tranquility, though the last remaining shipyard is still a close and audible neighbor.

Originally, the square tower would have stood here alone, a simple, solid fortress accompanied only by its functional gatehouse. When Sir Patrick Maxwell, a powerful friend of King James VI, inherited the castle in the 16th century, however, he had to add the living quarters which now join tower and gatehouse in order to house his wife and 16 children. The Castle passed out of the Maxwell family in 1694, after 200 years of ownership, and has since been bought and sold between private owners. Perhaps the most interesting resident was a ropemaker named John Orr, who, in addition to making rope, had a sideline trading in wild animals, which he bought from the ships docked at Port Glasgow.

With its stern-shaped south tower, Blackness Castle looks rather appropriately like a ship jutting out into the river.

Blackness Castle

Another castle with industrial connections, Blackness stands on the banks of the River Forth, with a clear view of the naval dockyards at Rosyth and the Forth rail bridge. With its stern-shaped south tower, it looks rather appropriately like a ship jutting out into the river.

During most of the 15th century, the Castle was appropriated by King James II as a prison, clearly for those prisoners who required more upscale accommodations. But below the Castle building was a pit which acted as a second prison for the less salubrious prisoners. A hatch leads down from the castle floor to this cramped, damp hovel which would have been flooded twice a day at high tide.

In the 16th century the Castle was remodeled and in the process greatly strengthened by James V, making it the almost impregnable fortress that it is today. Its south-facing walls are 16 feet (5 m) thick and punctuated with holes to allow artillery to fire out. The Castle entrance was constructed to be so convoluted and difficult to navigate that it hardly needed the beheading device which was installed to deal with any unwanted visitors who did manage to get past the outer gate.

History, Heritage, and Folklore

The people, the places, the customs, and the legends that make Scotland unique

Have you ever wondered what is meant when the Scots go "first footing" at Hogmanay? Or why they celebrate Burns Night by eating a sheep's stomach? Why is it that a Scotsman won't be parted from his whiskey? And what is all that tartan about? Scotland is a nation that clings firmly and with fierce affection to its many and varied traditions, even when their origin and purpose may long have been lost in the mists of time, and in this way it has ensured the survival of its unique national identity. The Gaelic language still thrives in many of the remoter parts, especially in the Highlands, and to ensure that the native language remains alive for the benefit of future generations, street signs are bilingual throughout Scotland.

Scotland's Celtic heritage furnishes its people with a treasure trove of stories, some of which may even, broadly speaking, be true, but others of which are best taken with a grain of salt. Since much of this heritage belongs to an oral, rather than a written, tradition, it is difficult to verify many of the legends that have passed down through the generations. And it is perhaps better this way: just because something cannot be proven, that does not mean that it is not true.

From prehistoric stone circles to modern feats of maritime engineering, from rowdy soccer fans to crucified saints, via lighthouses and a monster hiding in a lake, here we celebrate everything that makes Scotland Scottish.

Left: Illusion or reality?

Right: A more realistic portrait of Loch Ness. This deep freshwater loch runs along the Great Glen, a geologic fault line linking Inverness and Fort William.

Loch Ness

Shafts of sunlight pierce the surface of Loch Ness, and the elusive beast seems to rise from its depths. This may be an image more likely to emerge from a Hollywood studio than a Scottish lake, but strange beasts and mythical creatures have an important role to play in a country suffused with ancient Celtic folklore. They give us a glimpse of a magical past—a time when not everything could be explained away by science and technology, and they suggest powers at work which we cannot entirely control. This is appealing in a world so neatly packaged, and it goes some way toward explaining why so many people want the Loch Ness monster to exist.

So what exactly is the Loch Ness monster? A constant stream of tourists flows past the shores of this loch to see if they can find out and there have been around one thousand reported sightings of the "monster," but none have ever been officially confirmed. The legend reaches right back into the 6th century when it is said that St. Columba (the monk who is credited with bringing Christianity to the wilds of Scotland) commanded a monster who was terrorizing a local village to return to the loch from whence it came. This story has prompted many people over the years to seek out the monster in Loch Ness' depths, but it has so far managed to evade all that modern recoding technology can throw at it. Ironically, and frustratingly for some, the water in Loch Ness is exceptionally low visibility due to coloring from the high peat content in the surrounding soil. In some accounts the Loch Ness monster (fondly known as Nessie) appears to resemble a plesiosaurus, the dinosaur pictured here.

Right: Loch Ness on a bright, sunny day.

Below: A tranquil sky is mirrored on Loch Lomond.

Lochs

The peace and tranquility to be found on the shores of a loch is unrivaled. As the quiet waves gently lap the stony shoreline, the banks of mountains in the distance seem to enclose the water in a hallowed silence.

A traditional Scottish song, "Loch Lomond" celebrates the somewhat wistful romance of the loch:

"Loch Lomond"

By yon bonnie banks and by yon bonnie braes
Where the sun shines bright on Loch Lomon'
Where me and my true love were ever wont to go
On the bonnie, bonnie banks o' Loch Lomon'.

Oh you take the high road and I'll take the low road
An' I'll be in Scotland afore ye,
But me and my true love will never meet again
On the bonnie, bonnie banks o' Loch Lomon'.

Twas there that we parted in yon shady glen
On the steep, steep side of Ben Lomon',
Where in purple hue, the hielan' hills we view,
An' the moon comin' out in the gloamin'.

Oh you take the high road and I'll take the low road,
An' I'll be in Scotland afore ye,
But me and my true love will never meet again
On the bonnie, bonnie banks of Loch Lomon'.

The wee birdies sing, and the wild flowers spring,
While in sunshine the waters are sleepin'
But the broken heart it kens nae second spring again,
Tho' the woeful may cease free their greetin'.

Oh you take the high road and I'll take the low road,
An' I'll be in Scotland afore ye,
But me and my true love will never meet again
On the bonnie, bonnie banks of Loch Lomon'.

Left: Green tartan fabric.

" *The bonniest lad that ever I saw,*
Bonnie laddie, Highland laddie,
Wore a plaid, and was fullbraw,
Bonnie Highland laddie. "

Robert Burns

Traditional Scottish Dress

It may come as something of a disappointment to discover that the tartan kilt was not originally worn by Highlanders, but was part of the 19th century romantic revival of interest in Scottish clans. It was only in 1815 that the *Highland Society of London* began the process of naming and registering official clan tartans. The tailored kilt—or "philabeg" to use its Gaelic name—is a modern version of the "belted plaid," a single piece of cloth six feet long that was worn both around the waist and up over the shoulder.

Tartan cloth was originally intended as a decorative accessory to be worn over ordinary clothing. It made use of the limited range of color dyes available and was woven of the cheapest local coarse wool. The word "tartan" had nothing to do with color or pattern, but was a description of the weaving process: each thread passing under two threads, then over two threads.

The revival of interest in Scotland's past coincided with a boom in industry, particularly in the weaving industry. But it took a royal visit to set the ball rolling. When King George IV visited Edinburgh, Sir Walter Scott, who was managing the king's tour, made the grand pronouncement: "Let every man wear his tartan." This gave rise to a flurry of excitement as everyone rushed to get outfitted in their family tartan, creating plenty of work for the already thriving weaving and tailoring industries. From this point onward, the identification of a family with a particular tartan pattern has proven to be increasingly popular.

As is natural in these situations, the new popularity for tartans inspired the capitalist entrepreneurial spirit, and the market was exploited to the full, giving rise to the likes of hunting tartans, dancing tartans, and mourning tartans. The firm William Wilson & Son of Bannockburn had a monopoly in tartan making during the 18th and early 19th centuries. Their "Pattern Book" of 1839 boasts, for example, a Hunting Stewart design (the design is now no longer a hunting tartan, nor a Stewart tartan). The original tartan design is a regimental one called the Black Watch. It was once the only legal tartan and could only legally be worn by the Black Watch regiment. This idea of exclusive membership has proven to be a trenchant one, and over the years, the whole business of tartan designs became increasingly exclusive. Today, the only real taboo in tartan wearing is to make the mistake of wearing the Royal Tartan, known as Balmoral tartan—unless, of course, you are in fact a member of the Royal Family!

*Above: Three Scottish
soldiers in ceremonial
uniform.*

Right: The traditional Scottish dress for formal occasions.

Ironically, though the Highlanders themselves had not initially instigated the idea of family tartans, the wearing of tartans became associated with the turbulent clashes between rival clans and rebellions against the government. So severe was the problem that eventually the government banned the wearing of tartan. The 1747 Dress Act also banned the wearing of belted plaid and kilt—in fact, any form of national dress. A first offense earned six months in prison, a second offense a seven-year exile overseas, so it was no light matter. By the time the Act was repealed, Highlanders were no longer interested in wearing tartan. By then it had become a fashion statement in the upper echelons of English society, and any self-respecting Highlander wouldn't be seen dead in it!

Left & Right: Two views of the traditional Scottish Piper.

Bagpipes and Pipe Bands

Although the bagpipe is an instrument almost solely associated with Scotland, it actually originated in Iran and is still popular in the Arab world, as well as throughout Western and Eastern Europe. One of the clearest early references to a bagpipe suggests that the Roman emperor Nero was a player—he once threatened to play the bagpipes in public as a penalty for not winning a poetry competition, and one of his coins depicts the instrument. Some early Irish stone carvings indicate that the instrument had traveled to Celtic lands by the 8th century, and certainly by medieval times they were popular in the British Isles, most probably as a result of the Crusades that opened up the culture of the Arab world.

In Britain, pipers soon adopted the role of the traveling minstrel, or "troubadour." They roamed from court to court, carrying news in their songs and turning contemporary gossip into musical stories. A martial role also developed over time and pipers were soon employed to lift the spirits of marching troops with their rousing tunes. The post of clan piper, like the post of clan bard, was a hereditary one, passing from father to son through the generations.

A bagpipe consists of an air-filled bag—traditionally an animal skin, but more recently a synthetic material such as Gore-Tex—a chanter, the pipe which plays the melody, and the aptly named "drone." The construction of the bagpipe means that there is no easy way to stop playing mid-tune, which results in the endless long note or "wail" that is characteristic of bagpipes. Instead, grace notes, or embellishments, are written into the tunes to break up the phrases of music, and it is this technique that makes the bagpipe a difficult instrument to master.

The Pipe Band consists of pipers and drummers, and its origins are military. Queen Victoria's fascination with the Scottish Highlands and their traditions led to the formal appointment by the War Office of an official Pipe Major and five pipers for each regiment, which remains the official arrangement to this day. During the First World War, great numbers of military pipers were killed before the War Office banned the playing of pipes in the trenches. Nowadays, it is necessary to be a trained soldier in order to serve as a regimental piper, and the British army runs the Army School of Bagpipe Music and Highland Drumming, based in Edinburgh Castle, for the purpose of training piper soldiers.

Soccer

There are essentially two main soccer teams in Scotland: Celtic (pronounced "seltik," unlike in other contexts where Scots pronounce it "keltic") and Rangers. Together they form what is known as "The Old Firm," one of the fiercest and most notorious rivalries in British sports. Celtic has its roots in the East End of Glasgow and is traditionally a Catholic club, whilst Rangers—also Glaswegian—is traditionally a Protestant club. Over the years, the clubs have been blighted by the inflammatory sectarian behavior of some of their fans, and the managers have worked hard to promote religious and racial tolerance amongst the younger end of its fan base.

Celtic Football Club, the official name of the team, was formed by an Irish priest named Brother Walfrid as a means of raising funds for his charity, "The Poor Children's Dinner Table." In 1967, Celtic became the first Northern European team to win the European Cup, and what is more, they did it with a team consisting of entirely local players: every member of the team was born and brought up within a 30-mile radius of the team's stadium, Celtic Park in Glasgow.

Scotland has enjoyed less success as a national team, but they have a robust and loyal group of supporters known as the "Tartan Army." Unusually for visiting fans, the "Tartan Army" has won over the hearts of many foreign towns and cities owing to their boisterous good cheer and lively songs. The amount of alcohol they manage to consume has also been a welcome boost to many a local economy.

The Hogmanay tradition was probably introduced by Viking invaders in the 8th and 9th centuries.

Hogmanay

There is no doubt that the Scots love a good party, and the best example of this must be their traditional bringing in of the New Year, known as "Hogmanay." The tradition was probably introduced by the Viking invaders during the 8th and 9th centuries, but it has pagan roots going back much further, and the celebrations still retain some pagan elements, particularly in the importance of fire to represent the burning out of the old year. Today, the fire usually takes the form of fireworks, but in some towns they still swing giant fireballs in the Hogmanay parade.

The belief behind all the celebrations is that the year will only be happy and prosperous if it begins with a joyful break from the past. Consequently, tradition dictates that before the bells ring at midnight on December 31st, the house must have been thoroughly cleaned, the old ashes removed from the fireplace, and all debts repaid. Some more obscure traditions have now been abandoned, such as people dressing in cowhides and running through the streets while being hit with sacks. Nowadays, the celebration will certainly include music and dancing, drinking and eating—in Edinburgh and Glasgow there are all-

night street parties—and of course the singing of "*Auld Lang Syne*" (or "Days of long ago," to give it its modern translation). As soon as the last verse of "*Auld Lang Syne*" has been sung, it is time to go "first footing," or visiting the houses of friends. The idea is that the first people to step over your threshold in the new year will bring you either good or bad luck, depending on who they are and what they bring. According to tradition (and probably a relic of Viking days), a tall, dark, handsome man means good luck, while a woman or a blond-haired man means bad luck.

Left: Highland dancers present a bright array of colorful tartans at the 2006 Tattoo.

The Edinburgh Tattoo

Every year for three weeks in August, Edinburgh Castle plays host to the Military Tattoo, a spectacular display of marching bands and historical re-enactments, which celebrates with great gusto the pomp and glory of the military.

The triumphant spectacle ends on a more solemn note with a lone bagpiper standing on the castle battlements and playing a mournful *pibroch* to commemorate all his comrades-in-arms who have died for their country. But just as he has finished, the entire troupe of bands joins in with spirit-lifting fervor to play some of Scotland's most spine-tingling national songs.

> " *The glorious music of the pipes will set their hearts aglow.* "
>
> D. M. McKenzie
> *"The Bagpipes"*

Left: The cross of St. Andrew, the flag known as the Saltire.

The cross of St. Andrew, the patron saint of Scotland, characterizes the Scottish national flag.

Flags

It is St. Andrew, the patron saint of Scotland, whose cross appears on the Scottish national flag, raising the blood of many a patriot, but the history of his connection with Scotland is somewhat speculative. One of the Disciples of Christ, St. Andrew was a fisherman of Galilee and the younger brother of St. Peter, who is said to have founded the Christian Church. These two brothers were the first-called of the disciples, and Jesus famously said to them, "Follow me, and I will make you fishers of men." It is thought that St. Andrew traveled as a missionary to Asia Minor and Greece, and that in Greece he was crucified by the Romans on a cross of this shape.

Three hundred years after his death, St. Andrew's bones were taken by the Roman emperor Constantine to Constantinople (now known as Istanbul, the main city of Turkey). The legend goes that St. Rule, a Greek monk, was told in a dream to take as much of St. Andrew's body as he could to the ends of the earth. Scotland counted at the time as "the ends of the earth," and that was also where St. Rule happened to be shipwrecked, along with a tooth, arm bone, kneecap and some fingers belonging to St. Andrew. He washed up on the East Coast of Scotland, in the settlement now known as St. Andrews. Here, the relics were enshrined in a chapel, which later became the Cathedral of St. Andrews, a holy site to which medieval pilgrims flocked.

The whereabouts of these relics is no longer known, but it is likely that they were destroyed during the Scottish Reformation when Protestantism swept through the land, putting an end to idolatrous practices such as the worship of relics. Most of St. Andrew's remains are now in Amalfi

Above left: The Union Jack flag featuring the cross of St. Andrew (Scotland), the cross of St. George (England) and the cross of St. Patrick (Ireland).

Above right: "The Rampant Lion," the flag of the monarch of Great Britain in her capacity as Queen in Scotland.

in southern Italy, though small pieces have been handed back to Scotland over the years, first by the Archbishop of Amalfi, then by Pope Paul VI.

Another story concerning the flag tells how, while an army of Scots and Picts were in the midst of a battle against the Northumbrians, the leader of the Picts, King Angus MacFergus, saw a vision of a white X-shaped cross against the blue sky. So inspired was he by his vision that the Picts and Scots went on to win the battle. A memorial plaque marks the spot, in Athelstaneford, of the "Battle of the Saltire," proclaiming:

Tradition states that near this place in times remote, Pictish and Scottish warriors about to defeat an army of Northumbrians saw against a blue sky a great white cross like St. Andrew's and in its image made a banner which became the flag of Scotland.

Scotland and England joined in 1707 to form the United Kingdom of Britain, with King James VI of Scotland and I of England at its head. The flag of the Union Jack, combining the flags of England, Scotland, and Northern Ireland, was eventually adopted, to avoid confusion over which should be used.

Above: A graveyard featuring stone Celtic crosses.

The circle can represent the sun, which can in turn represent God. The joining of horizontal and vertical lines can represent the joining of heaven and earth, and may have been used to illustrate precisely this, long before Christ's crucifixion.

Right: The Celtic cross.

Celtic Cross

The design of the Celtic cross has origins far back in time, and the significance of its symbolism has been appropriated by various different groups. Christians might tell you that the circle is a symbol of eternity, signifying the endlessness of Christ's love, with the cross a symbol of the crucifixion offering unending salvation. A New Age pagan might tell you that the circle represents the sun, as worshiped by the Druids, or another, more daring, might tell you that it is a phallic symbol.

There is no definitive answer as to the meaning of the Celtic Cross. The early Christian sign of Christ, before the cross of the crucifixion became commonplace, was a *chi-rho*, the convergence of two Greek letters to form what has been simplified into the "fish" design. The Emperor Constantine, who made Christianity the official religion of the Roman Empire, made the *chi-rho* within a laurel wreath his emblem. This bears a resemblance to the Celtic Cross. However, the cross and circle are such universal symbols across all cultures that it is difficult to pin them down to one meaning. What is perhaps most important is that they are symbolic opposites: the circle is unending and it encompasses, or contains; the cross marks out a specific point and reaches outwards. The circle can represent the sun, which can in turn represent God. The joining of horizontal and vertical lines can represent the joining of heaven and earth, and may have been used to illustrate precisely this, long before Christ's crucifixion. Stone crosses that date back to the 6th century AD have been found on the Scottish island of Iona. The early Christians who carved them would already have a pagan heritage of design embedded in their culture. The two are not mutually exclusive; both lend their richness of meaning.

Right: Kilmartin Standing Stones, Argyll.

Left: The standing "Stones of Stenness" are situated on the Island of Orkney.

Right: Detail of Standing Stone.

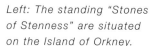

Neolithic Scotland

The Kilmartin Standing stones, one of many prehistoric sites around Scotland, are thought to have formed a sort of astrological observatory. Archeologists who carried out a thorough excavation of the site in 1973 have suggested that the formation of the stones could be used to track the movements of sun and moon, thus acting as a sort of calendar by which planetary predictions could be made.

On the island of Orkney, off the northern coast of Scotland, stands another stone circle known as the Ring of Brodgar. Situated on a thin strip of sloping land between two lochs, this ceremonial monument— a "Temple of the Sun"—is nestled in a bowl of land created by the surrounding hills. It would originally have contained 60 megaliths, but only 27 remain; some would have been worn away naturally by the elements, and others swiped by local farmers in need of a sturdy gatepost or a stone to repair a hole in their cottage wall. Those that remain standing, however, still form a "true" circle, one that is around the same size as Stonehenge, a similar stone circle located near Salisbury, England. It is thought that the Ring of Brodgar would have been part of a larger complex of ritual sites in the area.

A stone in the Ring of
Brodgar, Orkney.

Left: Shortbread.

> " *Freedom and Whisky gang thegither!* "
>
> *Robert Burns, "The Author's Earnest Cry and Prayer" (1786)*

Hospitality, food, and drink

The Scots are famed for their warm hospitality and their love of a festive occasion. Perhaps their most unusual culinary dish is the haggis, a sheep's stomach filled with a lamb's heart and lungs, all bound together with oatmeal and herbs. It is traditionally eaten on Burns Night (January 25) when it is ushered to the table accompanied by a bagpiper and ceremonially slashed open with a sword after a recitation of Robert Burns' poem, "Address to the Haggis."

Less dramatic (and less stomach-turning) is the humble shortbread. This cookie rich in butter is traditionally baked in a large round shape, which is then cut into triangles. It is a forebear of the New Year's cake which was shaped into a symbol of the sun, complete with

finger-pinched notches around the edge to represent the sun's rays. The first shortbread recipes date back to Elizabethan times, but it was probably being eaten long before that, since a butter-rich cookie is an obvious staple food to come out of a cattle-breeding region which has successfully mastered dairy farming.

Whiskey is inextricably woven into Scotland's culture. It was originally known by the Gaelic name of "uisge beatha," meaning "the water of life," which sounded to English ears like "uishgi"—hence "whiskey." Certainly, it has been greatly valued by the Scots over the years as a warming reviver to lift the spirits during many a long, cold winter. It would be unthinkable to welcome a visitor who has journeyed far with anything

other than a warming glass of the "water of life."

The first documented reference to whiskey comes in 1494 with a receipt for "Eight bolls of malt wherewith to make aqua vitae (the water of life)" supplied to one Friar John Cor. This quantity of malt would be enough to produce 1500 bottles of whiskey, so it is clear that Friar John had some efficient distilling machinery in place.

As whiskey grew in popularity during the 17th and 18th centuries, and distilleries became more widespread, the government levied ever more punishing taxes on malt and its end product. This was so resented by the people that smuggling became an acceptable practice, sanctioned even by the church: ministers were known to provide storage space for

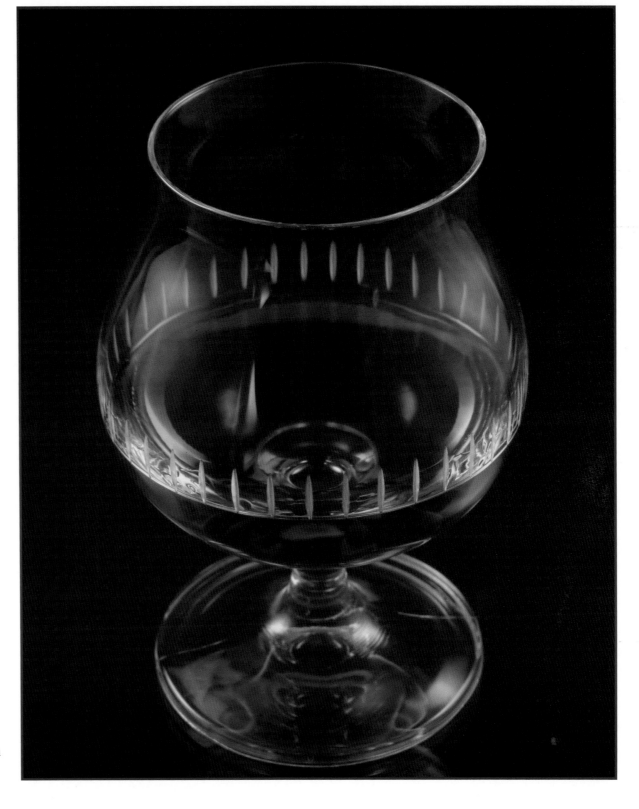

Below: Whiskey.

illicit whiskey under their pulpits, and the smuggled goods often traveled incognito in coffins. In 1777, there were eight licensed distilleries in Scotland and around 400 unofficial distilleries (not including those in the Highlands and Islands). Even though around 14,000 sets of illegal distilling machinery were being confiscated every year, still about half of the whiskey drunk in Scotland was tax-free. The government lost control of the situation to such an extent that in 1823 an Excise Act was passed limiting the tax on whiskey to the cost of a license fee, and smuggling eventually died out. It was around this time that grain was first distilled to make a lighter whiskey, and that blended whiskeys using malt and grain became popular.

Left: Toward Lighthouse, Dunoon, reflected in a rock pool.

Right: The lighthouse at Fortrose.

Lighthouses

For a country whose economy has always relied so heavily on sea trading, it is perhaps surprising that until the 17th century, Scotland had only one lighthouse: a coal-fired beacon which had been erected on the Isle of May at the mouth of the River Forth. But then came the Industrial Revolution and by the end of the 19th century, there were lighthouses all the way along the coast of Scotland. This flurry of lighthouse building was due in part to the remarkable skill of two Scottish engineers: Robert Stevenson and John Rennie, both pioneers in their field. It was Robert Stevenson (and his sons and grandsons after him) who built the majority of Scotland's lighthouses, most notably the famous Bell Rock light, standing 115 feet (35 m) tall. Lighthouses on offshore rocks had to accommodate their keepers, who usually worked four weeks on, four weeks off, as well as all the necessary equipment. Stevenson is credited with inventing the flashing light system, which prevents potential confusion with other coastal lights, such as the fires in lime kilns.

The cathedral city of Fortrose, on the Black Isle, boasts one of the lighthouses built by Stevenson. The waters beneath it are inhabited by seals and dolphins, and close by is a curious memorial to a Highland soothsayer, who met his end in a vat of boiling tar for speaking an unwelcome truth. The story goes that he told Lady

Seaforth, Countess Isabella of Ross, of her husband's infidelities with a Frenchwoman, which he had seen in a vision. His claim was later proven to be true, but it was too unpleasant a truth for the Countess' liking. With his dying breath, the ill-fated soothsayer predicted quite accurately the tragic end of the Seaforth family.

Above: The Forth Railway Bridge.

Right: Old railway tunnels at Falkirk.

Upon its completion in 1890 the Forth Rail Bridge was marked by His Royal Highness Edward, the Prince of Wales, hammering home a final golden rivet.

Railroads

It is hardly surprising that Scotland, renowned for its enterprise in engineering, is the home of the world's first major steel bridge. The Forth Rail Bridge was a massive undertaking in 1883 and its structure, based on the principle of a balanced cantilever, remains one of the marvels of civil engineering to this day. Three double cantilevers are yoked together by 350-foot (106 m) girders, and the entire structure is balanced by 1000-ton (900 t) counterweights along its outer edge.

The result is an imposing sight: the vast steel girders form a complex web of waves stretching across the river, and its bold red paint makes it all the more striking. The project was begun in 1883, and over the next seven years 4,000 men were employed in its construction, around 80 of whom were killed in accidents. Its completion was marked in 1890 with His Royal Highness Edward, the Prince of Wales, hammering home a final golden rivet.

Left: An abandoned steel hull on the banks of the Clyde.

Shipbuilding

The banks of the River Clyde are still lined with the ghosts of Glasgow's shipbuilding heritage. Abandoned carcasses like these are testament to a once-thriving maritime industry, now—like the hollow hulks that lie along the shore—largely rusting. The Clyde shipyards once produced the great transatlantic liners the *Queen Mary*, the *Queen Elizabeth* and the *QEII*, and ensured that Britain was kept at the center of the maritime stage.

When, in the 19th century, steamships began to replace sailing ships, Scottish inventors and engineers were at the forefront of the drive to advance and modernize the shipping industry. There were already shipyards all along the River Clyde, but wood was soon replaced by iron, and then by steel, and the waterfront became a hive of buzzing activity. Orders flew in from around the world, such was the reputation of the Scottish shipbuilders, creating thousands of jobs for local men—the ships, after all, needed not only building, but furnishing and carpeting as well.

But after the First World War, the paring down of the Royal Navy and competition from abroad meant that the Scottish shipping industry began to decline. Thereafter, the Clyde shipyards did not manage to keep up with modern developments in technology. They still had a limited building season due to weather conditions, while foreign companies built enclosed, all-weather yards. In addition, they were blighted by workers' strikes during the 1970s and began to gain a reputation for late delivery. Eventually the industry waned and the loss was felt not only in the economy, but in the deflation of the nation's spirit. Today, only five Clyde-built ships remain afloat in the world.

The Falkirk Wheel

Once the site of a battle which saw William Wallace defeated by the English troops of Edward I, Falkirk is now an important part of Scotland's industrial heritage, celebrated as the site of a state-of-the-art watermill.

The Falkirk Wheel, another awe-inspiring feat of steel engineering, is the world's first rotating boatlift. Its function is to transfer boats between the Forth and Clyde Canal and the Union Canal. These two canals have ensured the long-term industrial prosperity of Falkirk, which was famous for its ironworks in the 18th century. On the banks of the Forth and Clyde canal stands the historic Union Inn, a pub that has been frequented by generations of thirsty canal passengers.

*Left: A view of the
Falkirk Wheel.*

*How sweet to move at summer's eve
By Clyde's meandering stream,
When Sol in joy is seen to leave
The earth with crimson beam;
When islands that wandered far
Above his sea couch lie,
And here and there some gem-like star
Re-opes its sparkling eye.*

Andrew Park, "The Banks of Clyde"

Crofting

In addition to its reputation for industrial prowess, Scotland also has a rich agricultural heritage. The days of the traditional "crofters," who rented and farmed a small parcel of land on which they also lived, have largely passed, but their legacy lives on. The run-down huts that are scattered throughout the Highlands and Islands give us an impression of a simpler, self-sufficient way of life that came to abrupt end two hundred years ago.

The Highland Clearances of the late 18th and early 19th centuries displaced many of these crofters by putting a sudden end to the subsistence farming that was their traditional way of life. Many tenant farmers were effectively thrown off their land to be replaced by more profitable grazing sheep in an episode that has become notorious for its brutality. Some were forced to emigrate, but some landlords—who saw in these desperate men an opportunity for cheap labor—tried to prevent this. Nowadays, as a means of redress, crofters are offered some security by the Crofter's Act, which protects their use of common pasture and allows them to gain ownership of the land they farm.

A dilapidated crofter's hut.

*Left: Graveyard at
Melrose Abbey.*

*The Melrose Abbey also has more
mystical connection: it is said that
the body of the 13th-century wizard
Michael Scott is buried here.*

The Church in Scotland

Christianity has blessed Scotland with a fine heritage: the architecture, the music, the art and literature that are the legacy of its ancient monastic tradition have enriched the nation with their depth and beauty. But it is the incomparable atmosphere of concentrated tranquility in places such as Holy Island off the coast of Arran that is the real legacy of the Christian saints who first landed on the coast of Scotland.

The original Melrose Abbey, founded in 1136 by King David I, was the first Cistercian abbey in Scotland. Cistercians were a new order of monks, formed in reaction to the laxity of their Benedictine brothers. They still followed the Rule of St. Benedict, but more strictly, emphasizing personal poverty and strenuous manual labor. Their hard physical labor brought them economic success. In the abbey at Melrose they farmed the land and traded in sheep's wool, which afforded plentiful rewards. This, coupled with their appealing austerity, made the Cistercian order popular and it soon spread throughout Europe.

They were particularly famous for their agricultural success. There is a story in which the Abbot of Melrose once orchestrated his own "feeding of the five-thousand." Abbot Waltheof is said to have fed 4,000 peasants who flocked to the abbey and camped outside for a period of three months during the famine of 1148. Waltheof was revered as a saint for his miraculous acts of charity. There were four Cistercian

Left: Detail of ironwork leaf.

Right: Ironwork detail on the doors of St. Magnus Cathedral, Kirkwall, Orkney.

monasteries in Scotland by the time the inevitable happened, and their worldly success led to a decline in their spiritual purity.

The Abbey also has more mystical connection: it is said that the body of the 13th-century wizard Michael Scott is buried here. Amongst other miraculous feats, he is credited with having split the Eildon Hills beside the Abbey into three peaks.

Melrose Abbey was destroyed by three English kings over the years— Edward II, Richard II, and Henry VIII—and it never recovered from the final assault. But before that time, the heart of Robert the Bruce was buried in a vessel within the Abbey. Today an inscription marks the spot, declaring: "*A noble heart may have none ease if freedom fail.*"

St. Magnus Cathedral in Kirkwall, the capital of Orkney, is the most magnificent medieval edifice in northern Scotland. This red sandstone cathedral, built by the same masons who built Durham Cathedral in northeastern England, was founded by Earl Rognvald in honor of his uncle St. Magnus, at a time when this part of Scotland was still settled by Vikings. Actually, Rognvald instructed the building of this splendid building as a means to an end. He desperately wanted to get his hands on the earldom of Orkney, but the title was already occupied. In an attempt to wrest it from the control of the existing earl, he tried to win over the hearts of the people by promising to build them a church dedicated to their most revered saint Magnus, over whose grave holy light was said to shine. Rognvald kept his word, and eventually he got his earldom. More importantly, the people of Orkney got their cathedral, whose fine artistry they still enjoy today.

The sacred Three
To save,
To shield,
To surround
The hearth,
The house,
The household
This eve,
This night
Oh this eve,
This night,
And every night
Each single night.
Amen.

Alexander Carmichael,
"A Scottish Prayer" (1900)

A church hidden amongst
the trees in the town of
Peebles.

Right: A Highland bull on the Isle of Skye peers through his tangled hair.

Wildlife and Plant Life

The animals and plants that make their home on the heather-clad hills and rocky crags of Scotland

Scotland's natural environment contains a remarkably diverse range of habitats: its vast peat bogs, frozen plateaus, temperate rainforests and sodden salt marshes all harbor their own unique range of species. On the Isle of Skye, you might see the massive wings of the sea eagle as it arcs through the sky. In the clear, sparkling streams of the Spey Valley you might see a bright salmon leaping out of the water. In the Highlands, you might catch a glimpse of the noble golden eagle as it patrols the wide-open skies, or the majestic red deer, the "monarch of the glen."

The coats of highland cattle have earned them the affectionate name "shaggy coos" in some parts of Scotland.

Above: Aberdeen Angus calf.

Left: Highland cow.

Highland Cattle

Highland cattle are an ancient breed of naturally hardy creatures, which is fortunate since they have to endure some long and unforgiving winters. Nature has provided them with the means to withstand harsh conditions in their waterproof, shaggy coats and extra-thick hides. They will also eat a wide variety of scrubby plants that other cattle would not normally touch. Where most cattle merely graze on what is in front of them, Highland cattle will "browse" for food, even in the unpromising wilds where there is apparently little on offer. These skills have served them extremely well in their native conditions.

A group of Highland cattle is called a "fold," rather than a herd. The males have distinctive long, sweeping horns, which give them a look of ancient nobility, while the females are noted for being excellent mothers, calving trouble-free in the exposed outdoors and raising their young with expert ease.

Their coats have earned them the affectionate name "shaggy coos" in some part of Scotland, and they are prized for their easygoing natures and their ability to make the most of distinctly unfavorable conditions.

Highland cattle are prized for their easygoing natures... and their ability to make the most of distinctly unfavorable conditions.

Left: The Monarch of the Glen in mischievous mood.

The impressive antlers of the red deer stag known as the "Monarch of the Glen," have become an icon of the Scottish Highlands.

Deer

The red deer stag, known as the "Monarch of the Glen," has become an icon of the Scottish Highlands. The impressive antlers, which look so ancient and permanent, and give the monarch his regal crown, are actually shed and renewed each year. During the rutting season, the sound of their powerful, throaty barks and the clanking of locked antlers echoes through the glens.

The image of this majestic beast keeping watch over his Highland territory has been immortalized in the painting by Sir Edwin Landseer of the same name. Landseer was a child prodigy who was a close friend of Charles Dickens and became Queen Victoria's favorite painter. In 1824 he visited Scotland, ostensibly to visit Sir Walter Scott, but he failed to inform Scott of his trip and when he arrived at Sir Walter's door, he was not at home. Consequently, Landseer ended up touring the Trossachs on the way back to Glasgow. He was awestruck by the scenery around him, and he made countless sketches as he traveled through Scotland. His painting of a stag, entitled "The Monarch of the Glen," became immensely popular in Victorian times, encapsulating as it did the romantic vision of the Highlanders and their proud, territorial stature. Thereafter, Queen Victoria, who had a special place in her heart for Scotland, championed Landseer as her favorite painter.

The poet Robert Burns toured the Highlands in 1787 and came home to the Lowlands with a strong attachment to their native deer.

Robert Burns

"My Heart is the Highlands"

My heart's in the Highlands, my heart is not here,
My heart's in the Highlands, a-chasing the deer;
Chasing the wild-deer, and following the roe –
My heart's in the Highlands, wherever I go!

Farewell to the Highlands, farewell to the North,
The birth-place of Valour, the country of worth!
Wherever I wander, wherever I rose,
The hills of the Highlands for ever I love.

My heart's in the Highlands, my heart is not here,
My heart's in the Highlands, a-chasing the deer;
Chasing the wild-deer, and following the roe –
My heart's in the Highlands, wherever I go!

Farewell to the mountains, high-cover'd with snow,
Farewell to the straths and green vallies below.
Farewell to the forests and wild-haning woods,
Farewell to the torrents and loud-pouring floods!

My heart's in the Highlands, my heart is not here,
My heart's in the Highlands, a-chasing the deer;
Chasing the wild-deer, and following the roe –
My heart's in the Highlands, wherever I go!

" Deer Stalking with the Sutherland Highlander
seems an almost invincible passion.
His constant thoughts and dreams are about the
mountain corrie and the stag;
get him into conversation on any subject,
and by some means it invariably comes round
to deer and deer-stalking. "

Charles St. John (1809–1856),
sportsman and naturalist

Left & Right: The pink-purple heather that clothes Scotland's hills.

Heather and thistles share the honor of being botanical symbols of Scotland.

Heather

Heather and thistles share the honor of being botanical symbols of Scotland. Before the Scots even inhabited Scotland, the Picts who pre-dated them were already using heather to make ale. Legends tells of a Pictish king who had himself and his son killed rather than reveal the recipe for heather ale to their Viking attacker. In later days, the Scots used heather to thatch roofs and to make seaworthy ropes or brooms for sweeping out the hearth. In fact, heather's Latin name, *Calluna,* is derived from the Ancient Greek "kalluna," meaning "to brush." Its medicinal properties have also been celebrated: heather teas soothed coughs and nerves, and heather ointments treated arthritis and rheumatism. It has even been used to fill mattresses because the calming aroma was said to ensure a good night's sleep.

The Victorians popularized the idea that white heather was lucky: it was claimed variously that white heather grew over a fairy's final resting place, or grew on patches of ground where no blood had been shed. Queen Victoria herself described how her servant Mr. Brown "espied a piece of white heather, and jumped off to pick it." No Highlander would pass by without picking it, for it was considered to bring good luck.

But the heather most associated with Scotland is the pink-purple variety which lies in thick springy beds all over the hills. A traditional Scottish folk song celebrates its romantic allure:

"Skippin' Barfit Through the Heather"

As I was walkin' doon yon hill
It was in a summer evenin',
It was there I spied a bonny lass
Skippin' barfit through the heather.

Eh but she was neatly dressed,
She neither needed hat nor feather;
She was the queen among them a',
Skippin' barfit through the heather.

"Will ye come wi' me, my bonny lass,
Will ye come wi' me and leave the heather?
It's silks and satins ye will wear
If ye come wi' me and leave the heather."

She wore a goon o' bonny blue,
Her petticoats were a pheasant colour,
And in between the stripes were seen
Shinin' bells o' bloomin' heather.

"Oh young man your offer's good,
But see well I ken ye will deceive me:
But gin ye take my heart awa'
Better if I had never seen ye."

Oh but she was neatly dressed,
She neither needed hat nor feather;
She was the queen among them a',
Skippin' barfit through the heather.

The misty bens and heather hills,
The sombre forest trees,
The lonely glens and mountain rills.
The deep clear inland seas,
Still ever haunt the mem'ry
Like some familiar strain,
And wake the hope within me
That I'll return again.
TRUE hearts and strong limbs,
The beauty of faces
Kissed by the wind
And caressed by the rain.

Anonymous

Previous page: Sheep in the Glencoe Valley.

Right: A seal basks off the coast of Bute.

Glencoe sheep

Glencoe has always been the homeland of the MacDonald clan, ever since it was given to Angus og MacDonald by Robert the Bruce in 1308 as a mark of gratitude for saving his life. It is a fertile valley, with its sweeping hills creating a sheltered haven. The inhabitants have always shared their home with the tough mountain sheep who graze on the land and furnish them with meat, milk, and wool. It is a landscape said to be peopled by witches, fairies, and giants: Final, the mythical Scottish giant who defeated the Vikings, is said to hail from here, and even now local legend tells of a woman called Bean Nighe who washes her clothes in the River Coe nightly, and brings instant death to those who see her. Today, the Glencoe valley is a thriving tourist destination, popular for the wide variety of sporting activities on offer. But the tough old sheep are still here grazing on the land, reminding passersby of quieter, more barren times.

Seals

Common seals can often be found around the coast of Scotland, either basking in the shallow waters or hauled up on sandbanks and rocky outcrops. About 90 percent of Britain's 33,000 seals live in Scotland. They are particularly plentiful around the island of Bute, where they are often mistaken for rocks, until they stretch and wake up! Further out to sea, there are porpoises, dolphins, and even killer whales, but the seals patrol the shallows, sometimes—in their playful good humor—following walkers along the shore. The innermost of the Inner Hebrides, the island of Bute, is a remote and peaceful haven with a thickly wooded shoreline and rose-tinged sandy beaches.

Left: Geese on the grassland.

Geese

Migrating geese are often attracted to Scotland because of its abundance of wet grassland and peat bogs. On the Solway coast, for example, the Caerlaverock salt marshes play host to scores of barnacle geese in winter. They arrive in the autumn after breeding north of the Arctic Circle, and they fly in long lines, hooting a noisy chorus.

Thistles

When in bloom, thistles are festooned with mauve feathers, but out of season they show their true colors far more starkly. Scotland's national flower, the thistle is stiff and thorny with treacherous prickles. The flower now known as the Scotch Thistle was originally the badge of the House of Stuart. By 1503 it had clearly become a national emblem because Dunbar, the "Rhymer of Scotland," wrote his "The Thistle and the Rose," an allegorical poem which celebrated the marriage of Margaret, daughter of King Henry VII of England, to King James IV of Scotland. In his poem, he dreams that a beautiful lady who is the month of May conducts him to a garden where he observes Dame Nature summoning all the birds, beasts, and flowers in procession. The thistle represents King James and the rose, his bride-to-be Margaret.

Then called she all flowers that grew in field,
Discerning al their fashions and properties;
Upon the awful Thistle she beheld,
And saw him keeped by a bush of spears;
Considering him so able for the wars,
A radiant crown of rubies she him gave,
And said, "In field go forth, and fend the lave.

And, since thou art a king, be thou discreet,
Herb without virtue hold thou not of such price
As herb of virtue and of odor sweet;
And let no nettle vile, and full of vice
Mate him to the goodly fleur-de-lis,
Nor let no wild weed full of churlishness
Compare her to the lily's nobleness.

Nor hold thou no other flower in such dainty
As the fresh Rose, of color red and white;
For if thou dost, hurt is thine honesty
Considering that no flower is so perfect,
So full of virtue, pleasance and delight,
So full of blissful angelic beauty,
Imperial birth, honor and dignity.

Below: Thistle balls

The thistle found its way onto the national coinage in the time of James VI and remains there today. It is often deployed by poets to epitomize the national character: strong, resilient, not to be toyed with lightly, and of course, displaying a joyful burst of color when you least expect it.

The patriot Henry Scott Riddell does just this in his poem "Scotia's Thistle":

Scotia's thistle guards the grave,
Where repose her dauntless brave;
Never yet the foot of slave
Has trod the wilds of Scotia.

Free from tyrant's dark control—
Free as waves of ocean roll—
Free as thoughts of minstrel's soul,
Still roam the sons of Scotia.

Scotia's hills of hoary hue,
Heaven wraps in wreaths of blue,
Watering with its dearest dew
The healthy locks of Scotia.

Right: Sometimes the most inhospitable weather creates the most breathtaking sights: the simple beauty of a broken, snow-laden fence in the mountains of Glenshee.

Landscapes, Seascapes, and Cityscapes

From the lively, bustling streets of the major cities, to the quiet solitude of the glassy lochs; from the neat fishing villages of the Islands, to the untamed wilderness of the Highlands

The vast array of different landscapes which make up Scotland is unparalleled in its variety. From the lively, bustling streets of the major cities, to the quiet solitude of the glassy lochs; from the neat fishing villages of the Islands, to the untamed wilderness of the Highlands, there is always some fresh new sight to greet the eye.

For some, beauty lies in the rugged, windswept hills and the majestic mountains; for others in the huge open spaces; for others still, in the trickling peat-brown burns. These lands have played host to some of the most colorful—and some of the most bloody—chapters in history: dramatic scenes that have been played out in a variety of equally dramatic settings.

Left: Neat rows of fishermen's cottages in Cromarty.

Standing on the east coast of the Highlands, Cromarty has remained virtually unchanged since the days when it was a thriving seaport in the 18th century.

Cromarty, the Black Isle

Whitewashed cottages huddle together against the bracing coastal winds in Cromarty on the Black Isle. Standing on the east coast of the Highlands, Cromarty has remained virtually unchanged since the days when it was a thriving seaport in the 18th century. Humble fishermen's cottages still stand alongside the grand sandstone residences of wealthy textile merchants in a village that seems to be locked in a more gracious past.

Throughout its history, Cromarty has relied on its proximity to the sea for its livelihood. There were two peaks in its fortunes: during the 17th century when trade with Norway, Sweden, and Holland was at its height, and again during the 19th century when there was a boom in herring fishing. After that, it came to a dignified standstill, bypassing the modernization process that so many other towns underwent, until the oil boom of the 1970s once again raised its fortunes and enabled the renovation of its fine historic buildings. Today it stands as a testament to the gentle decorum of times past, and a haven from the hubbub of the traditional tourist routes.

Right: Hadrian's Wall—still standing after nearly 2,000 years.

The wall was built by 10,000 Roman soldiers, and the fact that it is still standing largely intact is a remarkable testament to their skill in building.

Hadrian's Wall country

Hadrian's Wall meanders through the rugged countryside of Northern England. The wall, which stretches 73 miles from Newcastle to Carlisle, once ran along the ancient Roman boundary between England and Scotland and thus marked the northernmost frontier of the Roman Empire. As well as making boundaries clear, it was also intended to prevent military raids from the wild tribes across the border. Certainly, this impressive and imposing symbol of Roman power would have acted as an effective deterrent in warning unwelcome intruders to keep out. The wall was, however, punctuated by gates, which it is thought would have enabled the Romans to tax goods which passed through in trade between the North and South. All in all, a useful piece of stonework, well worth the effort it must have taken to construct.

The wall was built by 10,000 soldiers, and the fact that it is still standing largely intact is a remarkable testament to their skill in building. Various Roman artefacts are still being found along length of the wall today. Its construction was instigated by the Emperor Hadrian when he visited Britain in AD 122 to consolidate the existing Empire, having failed to expand it farther north. Its purpose, he stated, was "to separate Romans from Barbarians." Today, the wall provides one of the most popular hiking routes in Britain.

Left: "Ring out the old,
ring in the new."

City life

Historic architecture meets the necessities of modern life in this scene of urban contrasts. Scotland's cities boast some majestic and historic architecture, but they also have their fair share of poverty and dereliction. Urban regeneration has been a constant process over the last two centuries, particularly in Glasgow.

In recent years, Glasgow has won various prestigious civic awards recognizing its turnaround from virtual slum to vibrant cultural city.

Glasgow—urban development

In the 19th century, tenements were built across Scotland to provide mass housing for the poorer residents of the city, such as its laborers and artisans. They were particularly prevalent in Glasgow, where the dense population was most in need. The tenement buildings were three to five stories high, with two to four apartments on each floor. The stairs and landings were communal areas, referred to as the "close" or the "stair," and the phrase "a good stair" meant that there were good neighborly relations in that building. Often there was a pub on the ground floor. Though originally designed as housing for the poor, these tenements are now sought after by more upscale clients, particularly young professionals buying their first home.

In Glasgow, urban renewal projects in the 1950s, 60s, and 70s cleared out the 19th century tenement buildings, which had fallen upon hard times and were now seen as slums. In their place came high-rise buildings, which only exacerbated the problem. Within a couple of decades, these high-rise developments became dens of crime and poverty. It is now recognized that the size and communal aspects of tenements were good for building communities in a way that the high-rise buildings simply were not.

During the latter half of the 20th century, Glasgow was in a slump, with large areas of poverty, unemployment, and general urban decay. However, it has picked itself up again, reinventing itself as a city vibrant with art and culture. The regeneration process, which still continues, has worked. Investment has poured into the city, enabling the restoration of its galleries and museums and the Clyde waterfront is now being redeveloped. In recent years, Glasgow has won various prestigious civic awards recognizing its turnaround from virtual slum to vibrant cultural city.

Left: Kelvingrove Museum and Art Gallery, Glasgow.

Glasgow—city of art and architecture

The Kelvingrove Art Gallery and Museum is one of Glasgow's highlights. This impressive sandstone palace, built in 1901 in the Classical style, is home to a stunning array of arms and armor, as well as a wide range of archaeological and artistic curiosities.

Glasgow is famous for the quality of its art and architecture. In the Victorian era, the city was blessed in two of its native sons: the talented architects Charles Rennie Mackintosh and Alexander "Greek" Thompson, who between them furnished Glasgow with many fine buildings. Mackintosh's crowning masterpiece is the Glasgow School of Art. His experimental, forward-looking style has earned him world renown, but it is Glasgow that benefited most from his genius. Influenced by Art Nouveau and inspired by nature, he was perhaps unique among architects of the time in that he took an all-inclusive approach, designing not only the building, but the furnishings and fittings inside it, down to the wallpaper and carpets; perhaps his most famous design is his elegant

high-backed chair. Rennie Mackintosh was primarily an artist, and he viewed architecture as "the synthesis of the fine arts." The Lighthouse, The Hill House, Willow Tea Rooms and Queen's Cross Church, among others, provide a lasting testimony of Rennie Mackintosh's prodigious talent, which was in many ways before its time and under-appreciated in his home city.

Alexander Thompson was another truly original architect, sorely neglected in his own time. He was nicknamed "the Greek" because his style was reminiscent of Classical Greek architecture, but he took the style to new places by his unconventional, modern approach which included the use of iron beams and plate glass and a focus on the idea of the horizontal, long before it became more commonplace.

Glasgow now has a reputation for fostering cutting-edge art and the city's many galleries include the Burrell Collection, the Hunterian Gallery, and the Kelvingrove Art Gallery and Museum.

Right: The newly restored Kibble Palace in the Botanic Gardens, Glasgow.

Kibble Palace

One of the modern architectural wonders of Glasgow is the newly restored Kibble Palace, an elegant greenhouse in the city's Botanic Gardens. This Victorian marvel in curvilinear iron and glass has been painstakingly dismantled, restored off-site in Yorkshire, and reassembled in place. During restoration, the entire plant collection, whose treasures include Australasian tree ferns dating back to the 19th century, had to be removed for the first time since they were installed in the 1880s. The fact that it has remained largely intact over the years, despite being constructed of potentially delicate materials, is due in large part to the aerodynamic design, which forces the wind to flow over and around the building.

The Kibble Palace was originally the private, home-built greenhouse of the Glaswegian engineer John Kibble. In 1872, he donated the building to the Royal Botanic Institution, dismantling it himself and bringing it up the River Clyde to the Botanic Gardens, where it was enlarged for use as a public venue. During Victorian times, two English prime ministers, Benjamin Disraeli and William Gladstone, were inaugurated as rectors of the University of Glasgow under its domed roof. Thereafter, it was further modified to make it suitable for the cultivation of plants, which has been its primary purpose ever since. Now that it has been restored, Kibble Palace will become an entertainment venue once again, as well as continuing as the home of many rare and delicate species of plants from temperate zones, such as Australasia, South America, and China.

Right: Coastal path, Isle of Arran.

The Isle of Arran

Around the bend of a coastal path, the worn rock face of the Isle of Arran rises up out of sea. Situated on ancient bedrock, Arran is home to Iron Age forts and Bronze Age stone circles. It is a place of mystery and great beauty, that has yet to experience the ravages of the modern world. The oval-shaped island, 25 miles (40 km) long, is often referred to as "Scotland in Miniature," owing to the fact that it combines the dramatic, wild scenery of the Highlands with the quiet decorum of the south. The north is desolate and unspoiled with excellent hiking. The route up to the Glenashdale Falls, for example, takes in a steady woodland climb, with thick, springy bracken underfoot and trickling burns all around.

Arran feels as if it is stuck in a time warp, but pleasantly so: it is quaint and old-fashioned in an effortless way. The seafront at Lamlash, for example, looks as if it belongs on a 1960s picture postcard. And there are still "front" and "back" cottages running along the shore, relics from the days when families moved out of their proper cottage into a "back cottage" behind it, so that they could rent their home out to tourists during the summer months. The back cottages look like hastily erected dollhouses, but inside they are actually quite cozy and perfectly serviceable for a summer spent mainly outdoors.

Opposite Lamlash you will find Holy Isle. The island is now owned by Tibetan Buddhists who run meditation retreats on the island, but there was a monastery here as early as the 13th century, so it has long been a sacred site. The Isle even harbors the hermit cave of the 6th century monk St. Molaise, complete with runic writing on its walls, and a spring whose water is said to have healing properties. The Buddhist community has set up the "Center for World Peace and Health," an environmentally sound building from which they conduct their courses, at the south end of the island. At the other end of the island, a community of nuns is undertaking three-year retreats, but the rest of the space is given over to the wild Eriskay ponies, Saanen goats and Soay sheep.

On the opposite side of the Isle of Arran are the King's Caves, where legend has it that Robert the Bruce watched a persistent spider try time and again to scale the rock face. It is said that the experience inspired his own determination never to give up his struggle for Scottish independence.

Above: A climber scales a snow-filled gully in Glencoe.

" *In the Gaelic tongue, Glencoe signifies the Glen of Weeping* **"**

Lord Macaulay (1855)

Large parts of the movies Highlander, Braveheart, and Rob Roy were filmed in the Glen and it is easy to see why: the breathtaking serenity of its sharp peaks and the colorful carpets of wild flowers in its foothills make it quintessential Scotland.

Glencoe

With its landscape of dramatic contrasts, Scotland provides an endless challenge to walkers and climbers. Here at Glencoe, a rugged region formed of massive boulders and crashing waterfalls, an intrepid climber scales a perilous, snow-filled gully.

Large parts of the movies *Highlander*, *Braveheart*, and *Rob Roy* were filmed in the Glen and it is easy to see why: the breathtaking serenity of its sharp peaks and the colorful carpets of wild flowers in its foothills make it quintessential Scotland. There are also vast tracts of woodland scattered with bluebells, providing a natural home to deer, otters, and pinemartens, while golden eagles can often be spotted soaring overheard.

It is difficult to avoid mention of one of the most shameful episodes in Scottish history—the massacre of Glencoe. When King William replaced James VII, some of the Highland clans were suspected of harboring loyalty to the old king. In order to secure his position, King William demanded an oath of loyalty from all the Highland clans, which had to be taken by 31ˢᵗ December 1691. Most took the oath, though some struggled with their consciences over it. The aged Macdonald of Glencoe took some time to come to his decision and by the time he traveled to Inverlochy Castle to take his oath, the place was deserted. He was required instead to travel the 70 miles (112 km) to Inverary Castle during rough winter weather, but by the time he got there, the deadline had passed. He took the oath, but an official of the new regime decided that the Macdonalds should be made an example of. With the king's backing, he ordered the slaughter of all men under 70 in the clan. This brutal task fell to Captain Robert Campbell as head of the Argyll regiment. The massacre was made worse by the underhanded way in which it was carried out: the regiment led by Campbell exploited the code of Highland hospitality, asking to lodge his regiment at the Macdonald castle. They struck at 5:00 in the morning and by then many of the clan had gotten wind of the plot and fled, but 38 were killed, and many women and children died as they fled to the frozen hills. The massacre brought bitter enmity upon the Campbell clan, and it remains once of the most appalling episodes in Highland history.

Right: The harbor front, Portree, Isle of Skye.

Portree, Isle of Skye

A patchwork of pastel cottages flanks the shoreline of Portree. A natural harbor, the fishing village of Portree is the capital of the Isle of Skye and the home of the Skye Highland Games, which are held here every year in August.

There are two possible roots of the name "Portree." Some trace its name to the Gaelic Port Ruighe or "port of the slopes," but others hold that it is rightfully—and far more poetically—Port-an Righ or "port of the king." This name is traced back to a visit by King James V when he was trying to garner the support of the island clans. There are other, more romantic, royal connections to the place. The Royal Hotel in Bank Street stands on the site of what was once MacNab's Inn. It was here that in 1746 Bonnie Prince Charlie said his final farewell to Flora MacDonald, the woman who is immortalized in a traditional song for having brought him "Over the sea to Skye." During the 18th and 19th centuries, a large proportion of the population emigrated to America from Portree—poverty, famine and over-population driving them away. It wasn't until a local laird Sir James MacDonald developed a fishing port here that a degree of prosperity began to return, and Skye islanders were able to stay put.

The harbor is certainly the crowning glory of Portree, with its picture-perfect cottages lined up along the shore, backed by steep wooded cliffs and surrounded by bobbing sailing boats. Who would have thought, looking at it now, that public hangings used to take place rather dramatically at the tip of its southern peninsula?

Kilt Rock, Isle of Skye

Skye's geology is most striking for its eccentric effusions: basaltic lava has created bizarre, ramshackle rock formations along the coast which look more like works of modern art than freaks of nature. Among them is the Old Man of Storr, a 160-foot pillar of rock which has detached itself from the land and juts boldly up into the sky. It has served as a landmark for sailors for centuries and it was only in 1955 that climbers managed to reach its peak. Another is Kilt Rock, which gets its name from the vertical lines along the basalt cliff face which resemble the pleats of a kilt. They also overlie deeper horizontal lines, giving the impression of an unusual natural tartan. This skirt of rock, with its deeply scored trenches, certainly gives a dramatic impression as it rises steeply from the sea, especially with the waterfall that cascades over its crinkled surface to the shore beneath.

Left: Kilt Rock, Isle of Skye.

The Isle of Skye

Skye is the largest of the Hebridean islands and the home of the warring Macleod and MacDonald clans, who each held an end of the island. Two castles whose ruins still stand today mark their rival territories. The MacDonalds made their home in the cliff-top Duntulm Castle at the northwest tip of the island. Local legend tells how the MacDonalds abandoned the castle in the 18th century following a tragic accident when a nursemaid let the baby heir of the MacDonald clan fall from a castle window to its death on the rocks below. The Macleod clan has inhabited Dunvegan Castle in the south of the island for over 700 years. The most precious family treasure still kept in the castle to this day is an ancient silken flag known as the Fairy Flag. It is said that a fairy gave the flag to the chief of the clan, claiming that it would guarantee victory in battle three times. It has been carried into battle twice so far and on both occasions proved reliable.

Perhaps the most bloodthirsty episode in the long-running feud between these two neighboring clans came in the 16th century when the MacDonalds set fire to a pile of brushwood at the entrance to a cave that the Macleods had hidden in, burning to death all 395 members of the clan who were sheltering inside. As revenge, the Macleods set fire to a church, killing the entire MacDonald congregation inside.

The most beloved of the MacDonald clan, and Skye's most famous daughter, is Flora MacDonald. It was she who helped Bonnie Prince Charlie escape certain death at the hands of the English following his defeat at the Battle of Culloden in 1746. Flora disguised herself as an Irish servant girl and transported the Prince over the sea to Skye in her own boat, from which he fled to France. She took a lock of his hair as a keepsake. When her part in the escape was discovered, she was arrested and sent to the Tower of London for a year, but was subsequently released. Flora lived in North Carolina with her husband for a while, but they eventually returned to Skye and she is buried in the graveyard at Kilmuir. A memorial penned by Samuel Johnson pays her fitting tribute: *"A name that will be mentioned in history, and if courage and fidelity be virtues, mentioned with honour."*

Left: A forest on the Isle of Skye.

Skye Boat Song
(Traditional)

Speed bonnie boat, like a bird on the wing,
Onward, the sailors cry,
Carry the lad that's born to be king
Over the sea to Skye.

Loud the winds howl, loud the waves roar,
Thunder clouds rend the air;
Baffled our foes stand on the shore
Follow they will not dare.

Speed bonnie boat, like a bird on the wing,
Onward the sailors cry,
Carry the lad that's born to be king
Over the sea to Skye.

Though the waves leap, soft shall ye sleep,
Ocean's a royal bed.
Rocked in the deep, Flora will keep
Watch by your weary head.

Speed bonnie boat, like a bird on the wing,
Onward the sailors cry,
Carry the lad that's born to be king
Over the sea to Skye.

Burned are our homes, exile and death
Scatter the loyal men.
Yet, e'er the sword cool in the sheath,
Charlie will come again.

Speed bonnie boat, like a bird on the wing,
Onward the sailors cry,
Carry the lad that's born to be king
Over the sea to Skye.

Ayr Coast, looking over toward Arran in the mist.

The Ayr Coast

The Ayr coast, which looks over towards the peaceful charm of the Isle of Arran in the mist, has been a popular seaside resort since Victorian times, but it has seen some turbulent days. The town was once a medieval port and played an important part in Scotland's struggles with the invading English forces in the 13th and 14th centuries. It was here that William Wallace set fire to the barns which housed 500 of Edward I's English soldiers. And it was in this same historic spot that Robert Bruce tore down the castle rather than have it occupied by the English.

> *York was, London is, but Edinburgh shall be The greatest of the three.*
>
> *Thomas the Rhymer (13th century)*

Edinburgh

Edinburgh is divided into an elegant Georgian New Town and a graceful historic Old Town. These tenement buildings on Edinburgh's Royal Mile are typical of the Old Town's genteel charm. Edinburgh prides itself on its old-world grandeur and has, in the past, had the reputation of a rather straitlaced spinster. However, in recent years, annual events such as the riotous Hogmanay celebrations and the arts festival, which applauds all that is avant-garde in the world of entertainment, have done much to dispel that image.

The hub of the city is the Royal Mile, the street that stretches from Edinburgh Castle to the royal palace of Holyrood House. Holyrood Palace was built in the time of James IV on the site of Holyrood Abbey, a 12th-century Augustine monastery. According to legend, the Norman Abbey was founded by King David I after a scrape with death. The story goes that he was out hunting when he was brought down by a stag; when it tried to gore him, he held onto its antlers. No sooner had he done so, however, than he found that the stag was gone and he was holding onto a wooden crucifix. As thanksgiving for his miraculous escape, he founded a church dedicated to the holy "rood" or cross. Rebuilt in the 17th century in the style of a French chateau, today the palace of Holyrood House is the official residence of Queen Elizabeth II when she is in Scotland, which is usually for a few weeks during the summer. Holyrood Park, in which the palace stands, is refreshing oasis of greenery amidst the bustle of the city. It consists of 650 acres of impressive mountains, freshwater lochs, marshes, moors and wooded glens.

It is said that there is no place on earth to rival Edinburgh during the Festival. Buzzing with a unique creativity and thronging with excited people, it is then that the city truly comes alive. In theaters, pubs, church halls, and tents across the city, dance troupes, string quartets, puppeteers, fire eaters, comedians, and jugglers do their thing. All aspects of the art world are celebrated, and the variety is simply endless. Many famous names made their debut at the Fringe Festival, which was initially a sideline to the main, more highbrow International Festival, but has since spiraled out of control and entirely taken over.

Left: Ruins of St. Anthony's Chapel, Edinburgh.

Edinburgh prides itself on its old-world grandeur and has, in the past, had the reputation of a rather straitlaced spinster.

St Anthony's Chapel

The ruin of St. Anthony's Chapel overlooks St. Margaret's Loch, silently guarding its secret. No one knows when this chapel was built, or why. In fact, nothing is really known about it, except that St. Anthony founded the first monastery in AD 250. There have been various conjectures about this chapel—some suggest that a light was hung in its tower to guide ships on the Firth of Forth, others that the spring which rises from the slopes below the chapel walls is sacred—but nothing is known for sure. Certainly, the mystery is part of the charm in the case of this speechless ruin.

Loch Tay stretches for 14 miles and travels through some of the loveliest scenery in Perthshire.

Left: The stark and haunting beauty of a tree-covered island rising up out of the morning mist on Loch Tay.

Right: A beautiful image of Loch Tay on a calm spring day.

Loch Tay

Loch Tay stretches for 14 miles and travels through some of the loveliest scenery in Perthshire. Its shores were once humming with activity, housing a thriving agricultural and industrial community in the 18th century, but during the land clearances of the 19th century, many of its native crofters were forced to emigrate to Canada to find work. The remnants of these farming communities, including a number of crannogs—houses on stilts— can still be seen in places along the shores of the loch.

The abandoned village of Lawers on the north shore of Loch Tay holds some mysterious stories in its ruins. They involve the enigmatic figure of the Lady of Lawers, was said to have been a Stewart of Argyll who married one of the lairds of Lawers, but no firm records of her existence can be found. All that is certain is that tradition holds her to have been a woman of immense wisdom whose prophecies always came true. Many of them were quite general, predicting the coming of the railways and of how writing would cause men's memories to fail, but some were far more specific. She predicted that when a tree which grew near the church reached certain heights, various things would occur: when it reached the height of the church gales, for example, the Church of Scotland being torn apart, and indeed that stage of the tree did coincide with the Catholic-Protestant split of 1843. She further declared that whoever cut the tree down would come to a tragic end. About 60 years ago, John Campbell, a tenant farmer, laid an ax to the tree and was soon after gored by his own bull. She also foresaw the social and economic changes that would take place along the shores of the loch and, though she spoke in riddles, her predictions were always very detailed and always highly accurate.

There is something about the lochs— perhaps the wistful sigh of the wind on their shores; perhaps their calm, reflective faces—that seems to inspire songs about lost love.

Here, in a song set on the banks
of Loch Tay, the singer's love of a
red-haired girl, his "nighean ruadh,"
is unrequited:

Loch Tay Boat Song
(Traditional)

When I've done my work of day,
And I row my boat away,
Doon the waters of Loch Tay,
As the evening light is fading
And I look upon Ben Lawers
Where the after glory glows;
And I think on two bright eyes
And the melting mouth below.

She's my beauteous neighean ruadh,
She's my joy and sorrow too;
And although she is untrue,
Well I cannot live without her,
For my heart's a boat in tow,
And I'd give the world to know
Why she means to let me go,
As I sing horee horo.

Her eyes are like the gleam
O' the sunlight on the stream;
And the songs the fairies sing
Seem like songs she sings at milking.
But my heart is full of woe,
For last night she bade me go
And the tears begin to flow,
As I sing horee, horo.

Right: Loch Cobbinshaw.

Below: A long-abandoned Scottish fishing boat.

130

Loch Achray.

Left: Loch Lubnaig in the Trossachs.

Right: Buchaille Etive Mhor, Glen Coe.

Loch Achray

Loch Achray is an exquisite sight, nestled in the heart of the heather-clad Trossachs at the meeting place of Highlands and Lowlands. Its mirror-calm surface reflects the thick woods, jagged mountains, and deep green forests that surround it. There is no more peaceful place to walk, cycle, or sit and reflect on the meaning of life!

Mountains

There are several mountain ranges across Scotland and the mountains themselves are divided into three categories: Munros, Corbetts, and Grahams, named after the people who compiled lists of each type. Munros are mountains over 3000 feet and a favorite pastime in Scotland is "Munro bagging," that is, climbing as many Munros as possible. Corbetts and Grahams are progressively smaller.

Above: The peak of Ben Nevis.

Right: The ascent of Ben Nevis.

Ben Nevis

A handful of walkers begin the winding, rocky ascent of Ben Nevis. Standing over 4,000 feet (1220 m) high, Ben Nevis is Britain's highest mountain, retaining its thick blanket of snow well into the summer months. Its soaring and perilous heights command a view of the entire Highlands on a clear day. On an exceptional day, you can even spot the coast of Ireland. But it is a long way to the top, and some less experienced walkers are ill-prepared for the sudden change in temperature. As a result, there have been more deaths on the relatively easy-going Ben Nevis than on the far more challenging Mount Everest. At the top are the ruins of an observatory built in 1883, which provides useful shelter from the icy winds whipping off the Atlantic.

Right: Bruar Falls in the Highlands, immortalized in Burns' poem.

Bruar Water

When Robert Burns visited Bruar Falls during his Highland tour of 1787, he commented that it suffered from a lack of trees, noting in his diary, "Exceedingly picturesque and beautiful, but the effect is much impaired by the want of trees and shrubs." To remedy the situation, he did what he knew best and wrote a poem, which he presented to John Murray, the Duke of Athole, through whose estate the Bruar flowed. It was entitled "The Humble Petition of Bruar Water," and is written as if from the river to the Duke:

Let lofty firs, and ashes cool,
My lowly banks o'erspread,
And view, deep-bending in the pool,
Their shadows' wat'ry bed:
Let fragrant birks in woodbines drest,
My craggy cliffs adorn;
And, for the little songster's nest
The close embow'ring thorn.
Would then my noble master please
To grant my highest wishes,
He'll shade my banks wi' tow'ring trees,
And bonnie spreading bushes.

The poem must have hit the right note, because the Duke followed its advice, planting his estates around Bruar water thick with the plentiful Larch and Scots Pine trees that we see there today. In fact, he became known as "Planter John" for planting over 15 million trees throughout his estates.

Right: Two boats in Stonehaven Harbor.

In the 16th century Stonehaven missed its opportunity to become a hub of trading when nearby Montrose seized the monopoly in trading wool. Instead Stonehaven became a "haven" for pirates plying the east coast of Scotland.

Stonehaven Harbor

The fortunes of Stonehaven Harbor mirror those of its fellows all around the coasts of Scotland, tied as they all are to the fishing industry. The early days of the harbor's life were not auspicious. In the Dark Ages, this small collection of fishermen's cottages was frequently raided by marauding Norsemen. Then, in the 16th century, it missed its opportunity to become a hub of trading when nearby Montrose seized the monopoly in trading the likes of wool. Instead, Stonehaven soon became a "haven" for pirates plying the east coast of Scotland, causing one 17th century tourist to record in his travel journal: "there is a small harbor which they call Steenhyve which serves only for pirates and picaroons. I take the liberty to call it 'stinking hive' because it is so unsavory." Nowadays, far from being unsavory, it is one of the prettiest harbors in Scotland. Its days of prosperity came in the 19th century herring boom. Money poured into the town and much of it was rebuilt, including a pier constructed by the celebrated engineer Robert Stevenson. The fishing industry gradually fell into decline, but Stonehaven has reinvented itself to suit the tourist industry, making the most of its picturesque shorefront.

Left: A view through a broken wall on the Shetland Islands.

Shetland Islands

The Shetland Islands are formed from the sunken stumps of the ancient Caledonian Mountains which, eons ago, would have stood as high as the Himalayas. Erosion and flooding have created the beveled edge which is so distinctive of these islands. Water is an intrinsic part of life here—you are never more than three miles (5 km) away from the sea, and the land itself is scattered with thousands of freshwater lochs. The sea has always been a source of food and employment, and until roads were built in the mid-19th century, was the only means of getting around. And with so much coastline, the beach is never crowded. As a result, it's always possible to feel that you are the only person around for miles.

Shetland is perhaps most famous for its miniature ponies, which can be as small as 28 inches (71 cm) high. The pony's long hair and thick coat make it more than prepared for the worst that the blustery Shetland weather can throw at it and its size, which is a classic example of evolution, enables it to shelter behind stone walls and peat banks. The ponies roam freely on the heather-clad moorland, subsisting on a diet of heather and seaweed. In the 19th century, they were shipped to England to work in the coal mines when the law first came in which prevented children from being sent down into the mines. The Shetland ponies were an ideal replacement, as they could fit in the low-roofed tunnels through which the coal carts had to be pulled.

A taste of Shetland is a taste of the past: it is quiet, old-fashioned and very much in touch with the elements. The traditional ways of life that have worked for centuries are still maintained. Boat builders still use the same techniques as their Viking forebears, and they turn out the same craft, which you can see racing over the waves during one of the jubilant summer regattas around the island.

Waves pound the shore beneath the ruins of a castle.

Right: The River Tweed meanders through the luscious green countryside of Peeblesshire.

" *We had a day's journey before us along the banks of the Tweed, a name which has been sweet to my ears almost as far back as I can remember anything...* **"**
Dorothy Wordsworth

River Tweed

Peeblesshire is a landlocked country in the middle of southern Scotland, but its lack of shoreline is more than compensated for by the lovely River Tweed which winds through its wooded hills. The town of Peebles is neat and tranquil, only really bursting to life once a year in June during the Beltane Fair, a celebration of the Celtic festival of the sun. The broad, tumbling River Tweed has various stories associated with it, some of them a little far-fetched, but certainly worth the telling. Local legend claims that the wizard Merlin—of King Arthur fame—is buried near the point where the Powsail Burn joins the River Tweed. Apparently, he was stoned to death by local villagers who feared his magical powers. Another tale hails from the 13th century when it is said that Thomas the Rhymer, a notable soothsayer in these parts, foretold how "When Tweed and Powsail meet at Merlin's Grave, Scotland and England shall one monarch have." On the very day in 1603 when King James was crowned monarch of England and Scotland, the river rose to a height it had never reached before and overflowed into Powsail Burn.

Right: A wide expanse of sea at Durness.

The village of Durness is so deserted that its surrounding waters are used for firing practice by the British navy.

Durness

Remote and isolated, the village of Durness stands at the northwestern tip of Scotland. It is so deserted, in fact, that its surrounding waters are used for firing practice by the British navy. Its shoreline is spectacular, however, with steep limestone cliffs and fine white-sand beaches. Its major attraction is the Smoo Cave, a sea cave with a waterfall crashing through its roof, which shows signs of human occupation stretching back some 5,000 years. In the graveyard of the ruined Durness Old Church is a memorial to a notorious 17th century highwayman who is said to have murdered 18 people by throwing them from the top of Smoo Cave.

Durness became renowned during the Highland Clearances as a village which did not automatically submit to the evicting landlords, but put up something of a struggle. Some of the local crofters were eventually cleared off the land, but not nearly as many as originally planned, and the Durness folk set an example to other Highlanders that resistance was possible.

Right: A pine tree forest in the Scottish Highland.

Left: Tigh More, nestled in the Trossachs. This magical building featured in the film The Thirty-Nine Steps.

Trossachs

The Trossachs translates as "the bristly land," and there could hardly be a more fitting description of the scenery around these parts. Sir Walter Scott set his novel *Rob Roy* in these loch-ribboned wooded hills. It fictionalizes—and in the process greatly romanticizes—the story of Rob Roy, the flame-haired, outlaw chief of the MacGregor clan. Rob Roy was third son of the clan chief; a cattle farmer who built up debts he couldn't repay and eventually ran away with stolen money. The Duke to whom he was indebted seized his property and as revenge Rob Roy went underground as a woodland outlaw, stealing cattle and destroying the Duke's property. Because he stole from the rich and gave to the poor, and apparently treated his victims with polite respect, his reputation became something like that of Robin Hood, which has of course been the main focus of storytellers.

It was in this region that Gerard Manley Hopkins was inspired to write his ode in praise of the wilderness, named after the Highland village of Inversnaid:

"Inversnaid"
Gerard Manley Hopkins

This darksome burn, horseback brown,
His rollrock highroad roaring down,
In coop and in comb the fleece of his foam
Flutes and low to the lake falls home.

A windpuff-bonnet of fawn-froth
Turns and twindles over the broth
Of a pool so pitchblack, fell-frowning,
It rounds and rounds Despair to drowning.

Degged with dew, dappled with dew
Are the groins of the braes that the brook treads through,
Wiry heatherpacks, flitches of fern,
And the beadbonny ash that sits over the burn.

What would the world be, once bereft
Of wet and of wildness? Let them be left,
O let them be left, wildness and wet;
Long live the weeds and the wilderness yet.

" Name not the land where the olive tree grows,
Nor the land of the Shamrock, nor land of the Rose;
But show me the Thistle that waves its proud head,
Over heroes whose blood for their country was shed! "

Andrew Park

"Scotland the Brave," which is one
of the country's unofficial national
anthems, is close to the hearts of
many Scots, celebrating as it does
both the fierce beauty of the land and
the indomitable spirit of its people:

"Scotland the Brave"

Hark when the night is falling,
Hear! Hear the pipes are calling,
Loudly and proudly calling,
Down thro' the glen.
There where the hills are sleeping,
Now feel the blood a-leaping,
High as the spirits of the old Highland men.

Towering in gallant frame,
Scotland my mountain hame,
High may your proud standards gloriously wave,
Land of my high endeavour,
Land of my shining river,
Land of my heart for ever,
Scotland the brave.

High in the misty Highlands
Out by the purple islands,
Brave are the heats that beat
Beneath the Scottish skies.
Wild are the winds to meet you,
Staunch are the friends that greet you,
Kind as the love that shines from fair maidens' eyes.

Towering in gallant frame,
Scotland my mountain hame,
High may your proud standards gloriously wave,
Land of my high endeavour,
Land of my shining river,
Land of my heart for ever,
Scotland the brave.

Above: An early morning mist rests lightly on the River Tweed.

" *In the highlands, in the country places,*
Where the old plain men have rosy faces,
And the young fair maidens
Quiet eyes... "

Robert Louis Stevenson

The sun breaks through to illuminate a snow-capped peak.

Useful Information

Heritage and Culture

The two most significant players in the heritage field are:
The National Trust for Scotland
nts.org.uk
"A conservation charity that protects and promotes Scotland's natural and cultural heritage."

Historic Scotland
historic-scotland.gov.uk
"Historic Scotland safeguards the nation's historic environment and promotes its understanding and enjoyment."

For those with a general interest in all things Scottish, there are various informative websites including:
scotsman.com
heritage-of-scotland.com
friendsofscotland.gov.uk

These all provide information on Scotland's heritage and culture and are suited to the general enthusiast.

Archaeology

For those interested in Scotland's archaeology, the following sites provide a wealth of informative and interesting material:
scottisharchaeology.org.uk
scotlandsculture.org.uk

Both tell you how to get involved in various projects and offer resources for further research.

Government and History

scottish.parliament.uk/home.htm
The Scottish Parliament, which meets in Edinburgh, is responsible for legislation that applies specifically to Scotland.

bbc.co.uk/scotland/history/
The BBC's site includes a wealth of information on Scottish history.

Tourism

For those planning a visit, the official website of the Scottish tourist board is:
visitscotland.com

The Scottish Highlands Tourist Board site.
visithighlands.com

Clan ancestry

For those interested in tracing their Scottish ancestry, or finding out more about the clan to which they belong, there are a host of useful websites, among them:
scotsclans.com
electricscotland.com
cosca.net (Council of Scottish Clans and Associations)

scotlandspeople.gov.uk
An official government site with genealogical data for family and clan research.

The web directory for all sites related to Scotland is:
scotland.org.uk

Index